Connections & Reflections

Mothers & Daughters
In their own light, In their own words

Connections & Reflections

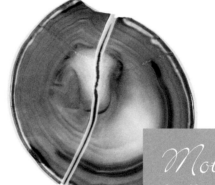

Mothers & Daughters
In their own light, In their own words

Catherine **Koemptgen**

Pfeifer-Hamilton Publishers
Duluth, Minnesota

Pfeifer-Hamilton Publishers
210 West Michigan
Duluth MN 55802-1908
218-727-0500

Mothers & Daughters: In Their Own Light, In Their Own Words

Additional credits
page 30—photo by David Arvold
page 40—excerpt from "If the Weather Came Inside" by Gloria DeFilipps Brush, 1980
page 100—poem by Ann Niedringhaus, published with permission of author

Printed by Doosan Dong-A Co., Ltd.
10 9 8 7 6 5 4 3 2 1

Editorial Director: Donald A. Tubesing
Project Coordinator: Heather Isernhagen
Art Director: Joy Morgan Dey

Library of Congress Cataloging-in-Publication Data

Koemptgen, Catherine.
Connections & reflections : mothers & daughters, in their own light, in their own words.
144 p. 20 cm.
Photographs by Catherine Koemptgen and excerpts from interviews
between her and several mothers.
ISBN 1-57025-147-9
1. Mothers and daughters—Case studies. 2. Mothers and daughters—
Pictorial works. I. Title. II. Title: Connections and reflections.
HQ755.85.K623 1997
97-21098
CIP
ISBN 1-57025-147-9
306.874'3—dc21

Printed in Republic of Korea

To my husband, Joel, and our daughters, Melissa and Andrea,
for their love and support

Special thanks to . . .

    Rosemary Ackley Christenson

    Ruth Strom-McCutcheon

    Adele Yorde

for their invaluable assistance.

Connections

Every morning before school, I French braid my daughter's hair.
With slow, sleepy fingers I separate and weave, separate and weave.
Silently, I gather the strands until they sit, just so, at the nape of her neck.
Then, still in silence, I place both hands on her head, praise the day,
and send her off.

While my daughters were in their teens, I grew my hair into a long braid. It was a small, symbolic gesture, honoring this ritual of quiet communion. When the early years ended, and my children were no longer by my side, I hoped to find comfort in repeating with my fingers the rhythms I knew so well.

We stood together on the brink of change. As they moved into adulthood, certain parental responsibilities would be replaced with freedoms I had forgotten existed. My mixed emotions—sadness, pride, relief, and anticipation—had no venue for expression. No official ceremony addresses this important, but largely unheralded time in a mother's life. I longed for a commemorative way to acknowledge and celebrate this universal passage.

As I looked around, I noticed mothers and daughters everywhere; in cars, shopping together in stores, and at home, cocooned in privacy. What did I know of their lives? What were the dynamics of these intensely interwoven relationships? How did they compare with mine?

Connections

As an artist, as well as a mother, I wanted to learn more. For three years, I photographed mothers and daughters. "Taking portraits," a term which implies a giving up or a loss of something, didn't interest me. Shared ownership of the creative process did. The portraits were freely and mutually "entered into" rather than "taken." Each photo session, as a collaboration, had a unique resonance. Once we began to work together and to trust this process, the portraits revealed themselves.

Photographing mothers and daughters in their own space had its challenges. Timing, particularly in the case of long distance relationships, busy schedules, light in a northern climate, and snowstorms were problems to be solved. The participants agreed to simple attire; no eye glasses or jewelry to create detractions. My format and equipment were as non-obtrusive as possible: natural light, a camera, a lens, and a tripod.

Despite my preference for simplicity, I found myself drawn to the many details that personalized each home. Women have always found creative ways to validate their life experiences, often preserving and displaying what has special meaning. Each new situation presented an opportunity to appreciate items of personal history. The "refrigerator art," toys,

Connections

quilts, scrapbooks, photo albums, and boxes full of "stuff" were the touchstones of their mother-daughter connections.

After the final portrait session, I invited the participants to move into an informal interview process. I am grateful for their honesty, insight, and humor. With selected mementos in hand, we sat at my round oak table of twenty years; the table of carved pumpkins and spilled milk, of laughter, anger, tears, and joy. Coming to the table, as mothers and daughters, we named the things that matter most. It was a fitting place to be.

Our best efforts to love and understand each other, one generation of women to another, are at times, imperfect; such is the nature of sacred work. This communal photo album of portraits, mementos, and recollections celebrates what is both ordinary and remarkable about mothers and daughters. Our faces map our humanity. And the specifics of our lives—the details—help us to discern the universals of human experience. Here are the revelations of those who journey beside you.

Catherine Koemptgen
October 1997

Linda

I can just look at this child and start to laugh. "Why are you laughing at me?" she will ask. It's just the memories, especially the incidental moments. For example, neither one of us can carry a tune, but sometimes I'll play the piano and Sarah will sing. It's really a terrible combination, but we have such a good time!

It's what goes on minute-to-minute that builds a relationship. Over the years, we must have put a thousand puzzles together, sharing what I would call unhurried, quantity time. Granted, I've had quality time with Sarah that is priceless, but quantity time, from silly to not-much-fun, is just as important. Everything counts. When you look back, it's stacks of incidental moments that make a lifetime.

It was expected from a very young age that all the children would give back to the community. Sarah delighted in it. We volunteered at the food shelf, the soup kitchen, the nursing home, and through the church. She never saw it as an obligation. It was just part of being a human being.

Danette

At five minutes old, she was wrapped in a blanket and placed in my lap. I thought to myself, "So this is who I've been carrying! Now what do most mothers do? Count fingers and toes." So, I undressed her and made sure everything was in place.

I think there was an instant bond with this new person, this new entity, but I don't think I *loved* her just yet. That had to grow. During the ten years prior to her birth, I had lived a professional's life. I wasn't around children. Those first months were a special time and a struggle. I went from complete control of my life to having my life controlled completely!

Jordan was born in September, and I returned to work in January. I had the *work* world and the *home* world. Though I loved Jordan, there was never any question whether I would return to work. For me, work was something I wanted and needed to do. Giving up my career wasn't an option. I was used to a working mom. Most of the women in my family worked. You went to school, you got your education, you had a family, but you also worked outside the home. That pattern filtered down through the generations.

Our name bands from the hospital stay connect me to that peaceful, tranquil time when I first met Jordan. I enjoy taking them out and looking at them.

Somehow I wanted to get my father's name, Dan, into our daughter's first name. After months of indecision, it occurred to me that "Jordan" met the requirements. I liked the idea that it was gender neutral, especially for the business world. When people see the name Jordan, they more than likely are going to think of a man and, to some extent, that might help get her foot in the door. I think names mean a lot. Jordan is a very strong name, and my Jordan is a very strong person. Her name suits her.

14

Berni

Every year I marked all the children's birthdays on the calendar. Each child had her own color. Teri was too little to read, but she could recognize the number seventeen. One year, she went through the calendar and marked "Teri" by every seventeen so we wouldn't miss her birthday. Being the youngest of six, she probably figured she might get lost in the shuffle.

Children are born with their own personality. It can't be drilled into them. You might smooth an edge, but you don't change that personality. When they took Teri's picture in the hospital, she had this look as if to say, "*Why* are you bothering me?" She came into this world determined to lead her life the way she wanted to.

Teri started hockey because her brothers played. Her brothers told her, "Girls are dumb, girls are stupid," so, of course, she always wanted to be a boy. She would wear her brothers' shirts. We were in a store one day and someone said, "Oh, your little boy is so cute!" I corrected her, "No, this is my daughter, Teri." When the woman walked away, Teri asked, "Why'd you tell her I was a girl?"

Julie

After our youngest daughter, Inger, died in a
skiing accident, Brita's maturity level changed.
She became an old woman. She wonders how
she ever went off to college that fall. She went
there with no one knowing what was wrong
with her—that her only sister had died. In our
grief, we became each other's woman friend,
the one who knew the depth of pain in the
other, deep down in her gut.

*I taught Brita how to can, a
tradition passed on to me from
my mother and mother-in-law.*

*Bunchberries cover the floor of the forest at the cabin.
That's a place where we both find
an enormous sense of peace.*

Kathy

In Korea, on the one hundredth day after a child is born, relatives gather to formally name the child. We named our daughter Stephanie, it means "crowned one."

Stephanie's Korean name is pronounced *bo-lahm*. It means to arrive at a place of clarity and worth through intense effort. That is how we began, with nothing but struggle. Her name was given to her by her great-grandfather. In his letter, he welcomes her as the "first of the first child."

As is the custom, on her Hundredth Day Birthday we placed a pencil, a string, and money within her reach. Whatever she grasped first would reveal her future. Stephanie chose the pencil, a symbol of scholarship. We were pleased. In Korea, the teacher or professor is of the highest regard.

We have never had anyone take care of our children. Stephanie has always been in the store with us. When there are no customers, we play hide-and-seek. For our family, work and play are not separate. Playing tag, stocking shelves, stacking blocks, reading a book—all parts of each day together.

Adu

My mother, my grandmother, and I lived in a German Displaced Persons Camp for six years—from age three through nine. We lived in barracks on a converted U.S. Army base, several families in each room, with brown paper partitions. Privacy? No one had any. But, under the bed, my grandmother stored a box of treasures which she had brought from Estonia. The box contained a green velvet dress, some shoes, and a silver ladle. One day, she pulled out the box and out jumped all these little pink mice. I remember the sight of her, banging the floor with the ladle as she tried to strike the mice. But it was too late. There was nothing left of the dress; the mother mouse had shredded the velvet to make a nest. The ladle has been passed to me.

I wonder why I gravitate to a time that was so long ago? It was a time when I really thought the world revolved around her. My mother was everything . . . she was the authority, she was the most beautiful woman in the world. She was my mother, my source of information. She had all the answers to any questions I asked. After we came to the United States, that changed. Since I learned the language a lot quicker, as children do, I was able to explain things in Estonian that my mother did not understand in English. I should have been pleased. I was not. I liked it better when my mother was able to answer every question I asked. I did not want the roles to reverse. They reversed too early.

It is ironic—years later we are still mother and daughter with a language barrier. She speaks Estonian at a level that I do not. I speak English at a level she does not. I can say, "I am painting a new picture," in Estonian, but I cannot tell her about the philosophical or formal concerns that drive my passion. I could tell her in English, but somehow that feels like a betrayal. Somehow it seems more important to speak Estonian than to be completely understood.

Kay

Sewing for Katia has been a strong bond between us. It has allowed me to pass on values beyond how a person *looks*. I wanted to make sure she realized that there is no substitute for a beautiful soul.

I've made most of her dresses, especially prom dresses, starting with Katia's own drawings. Sometimes she would come up with designs that were totally inappropriate. Shopping for patterns and material plus fitting sessions became our backdrop for important conversations. What was her image of herself? What was my image of her? Where did the truth lie? Usually somewhere in between.

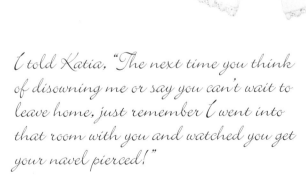

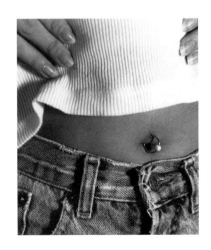

I told Katia, "The next time you think of disowning me or say you can't wait to leave home, just remember I went into that room with you and watched you get your navel pierced!"

Joan

Learning to be a single parent included certain realizations and
adjustments. I remember one incident in particular that happened soon
after I returned to full-time teaching. As a first grader, Molly prepared a
display about agates for a school fair. On the way to class, her favorite, a
sliced agate, fell and broke. Her older sister, Gina, called me at work. Molly
was sobbing in the background. How I wanted to be there, at that moment,
to make it right. But there was nothing I could do.

I promised my girls that once I became self-sufficient with a teaching job,
we would go to Disney World. That goal became a personal proving
ground. I kept my promise. Grandma came too. We had a wonderful time!

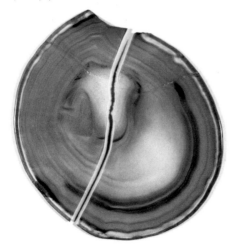

I don't know of any child who wants her
parents to get a divorce. Kids always live
with the dream that parents will reconcile.
That's what Molly's reality was. She held
on to the ideal. And, in a way, I think
that's good. I want to discourage my children
from moving in and out of marriages. I want
them to know that family is the core.

Anita

Even though Shefali is of East Indian descent she doesn't feel particularly different from any of the other kids at school. She thinks of her dad and me as really "different" because we were born in India. So *we're* different, *she* isn't! I get a kick out of it.

My school experience was very different from Shefali's. I lived in an all-girls boarding school in India from the age of ten until I was eighteen. The school dress code required that hair be tied back, shoes shined, socks worn to a specific height, and the uniform be pressed each morning. Beds had to be made and covers tidy. I learned a type of discipline that is unfamiliar to my daughter. In fact, Shefali never makes her bed! I'm not worried. I don't expect the same from her because our life experiences are not the same.

Tamera

Eva and I share a love of fantasy and drama. As an adolescent, Eva transformed her Barbie dolls into fantasy creatures. When I played with dolls as a child, I was never separate from the doll. I was the doll. We were one fantasy.

Eva

My inspiration for the dolls came from the dogs, cats, goats, chickens, horses, ferrets, and parakeets we raised together. The fantasy dolls hung in my room for a long time. When I moved away from home, I gave them to my mom.

Tamera

At times, I tried to fit Eva into a round hole when she was a square peg. I wanted her to do things *my* way. It never worked! We are both nonconformists but, of course, in different ways.

Eva

To be perfectly honest, Mom and I get along really well because we're no longer living in each other's backyard! We're so much alike, we clashed. The distance between us has improved our relationship immensely.

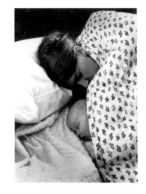

Judith

I thought I couldn't be more sleepy than when I was a medical intern
with an every-other-night rotation. But almost from the moment
of birth, Virginia was such an awake baby. The first three months,
I spent hours and hours just rocking her. I think I've analyzed every
turtle, every color pattern in her blanket. Virginia would take my
stethoscope and examine Big Blankie as if it were
a real person. I must have washed it a million times.

Virginia had a mind of her own,
but she was very sensitive to criticism.
I let her dress herself because she
knew exactly what she wanted to wear.
She would choose strange outfits and I would let her
wear them. It was easier that way. Some things are
important, and some things aren't. Sometimes
I would look at her outfit and cringe. But she thought
she looked good. I guess I thought that was more important.

Adele

When Amy was a baby, I wanted to buy her a doll that would honor the ethnic diversity in our family history. Twenty years ago there were no Native American dolls, but I found Lizzie. I believe ethnic diversity is a test— a test on this earth to see whether we can accept other people.

Lizzie comes from our past but she's also in our present. As a little girl, Amy always kept Lizzie close by, especially during storms. Amy had a fear of thunder and lightning. During a recent tornado warning, Amy's daughter Myrissa had the same need. She grabbed Lizzie.

Sharon

Sometimes I ask myself, "Are we too close?" But I think it's a stage, part of the natural process. I love every minute of her childhood, but I know she can't stay a child forever. And I wouldn't want her to! My baby has been given to me to raise to adulthood so that she can have her own life, not so I can wrap my life around hers. Although children never leave us emotionally, they do leave. I saw it happening when she took her first step. She stepped away! I work really hard to maintain my own life and personhood so when that time comes, it won't be so difficult. Bit by bit, life and God are preparing me for that day she walks out of our house.

The day I found out I was pregnant, I thought through Nicole's whole first year of life, especially day care. People cannot fathom what it means to entrust a child to someone else. Her care, well-being, and safety were foremost in my mind. I knew I'd only be as good an employee as I was comfortable emotionally with her care. It's unbelievable that some institutions in our society don't realize the importance of child care and how it impacts women. That support system is absolutely essential.

Carolyn

As the oldest of six children, I valued time alone with mom. I actually looked forward to doing the dishes. Mom would usually wash, and I would dry. Under the pretext of our chores, we talked about all kinds of things.

Gert

She was my big helper . . . always. With ropes and buckets tied to our waists, we would go cherry picking at a nearby fruit farm. Carolyn loved climbing up high. The biggest and ripest cherries were at the top.

Mother-daughter dresses

I was young right along with her. In the summer, we jumped rope and swam in the gravel pit behind our house. With winter came sledding. We raced down the hills like the dickens!

Melanie

Mom liked to end her work day with a cup of tea.

Late afternoon was a time when I knew I could talk to her.

After school, while she was cooking dinner,

or even when she was in the bathtub,

she was willing to talk.

I could ask her anything

over a cup of tea.

> *She taught me that I could laugh at myself.*
> *She taught me that I could be proud of myself.*
> *She helped me to love myself.*
> *ι college Mom was cool enough to go out with*
> *she even slept in my loft once.*
> *She was the one who finally asked me,*
> *"Meli, why are you taking organic chemistry?*
> *d "Have you ever thought about youth ministr.*
> *Mom is really wise, you know.*
> *When I decided to go to Africa she was quiet.*
> *med her on Thanksgiving Day that I might stay*
> *she was even more quiet.*
> *My friend lets me discover things on my own.*
> *n I have decided to marry and begin my own j*
> *she supports me*
> *by getting to know my fiancee.*

card by Melanie

Mom,
   Here are your choice selections for your b-day

(1) endless hugs + kisses
(2) A conversation on organization, a session for learning how to organize + you teaching me how too! you pick your 1 hr. 2x blocks in a weekend this or next to share with me your skills
(3) breakfast in bed for 1 week
(4) clean room for 2 weeks straight
(5) dinner every weekend night for 2 months (when possible)
(6) I set the table 1 month + wash the dishes (homework permitting)
(7) no hun, hun for 3 years
(8) On phone for only 1/2 hr a night for 1 week
(9) I make a diet-planner for you complete w/ exercise plans for summer.
(10) I send you + dad to dinner (yes, I pay)
(11) endless kisses
(12) flute piece every night for 2 weeks

pick 2 numbers.

I pick #'s 1 (amended) + 12 + 2
_____
Signature

Perhaps one day I'll ask
the weather to come inside.
We could have different weathers
in different rooms, special places
for special weather events.
First, for breakfast, clouds over
cereal: long puffy layers,
not too close to the ceiling.
When our oatmeal is eaten
we'd stand up, our heads
in the clouds.

from "If the Weather Came Inside"
by Gloria

Helen

When the swastika and "Kill Niggers" graffiti first
appeared on our house and sidewalk, Kai was too
young to know what it meant. It happened again a
few years later while we were away. She was confused.
I told her, "Some people do things like that,
most people don't."

Occasionally, there were cruel taunts from
neighborhood kids. Once it happened, I called the
parents of the children involved. They brought their
children to our door and apologized to me and then
to Kai. If there was a problem at school, I went
straight to the teacher or the principal. Being a
teacher myself, I knew how important it was. I didn't
necessarily tell Kai when I went. I was her advocate
behind-the-scenes. You can't ignore, yet you can't
hold anger and resentment. I had to teach her
tolerance. It's a hard thing to do. It is so sad
that we have to prove ourselves again and again.

Stephanie

Having a large family around me means that I'm not alone, that I'm not
by myself. As a child, I basically stayed home and took care of my siblings.
I started having kids when I was fifteen. Larissa is the second oldest
of seven children. I have always wondered what my life would be like
without them. It's not that I wish I didn't have these particular children.
But what else could I have accomplished? Where would my life be?

Dee Ann

We both have a passion for sports. I coached Shara in soccer
from third grade on. When her father and I separated,
our roles reversed. Shara became the coach. I heard my own
words of encouragement repeated back to me. "Atta girl!"
when I did something right. "You have to take risks!"
when I had my doubts. If I failed, Shara would remind me,
"There are no such things as mistakes, only lessons learned.
Besides, in fifty years, Mom, who's gonna know the difference?"

*Like the dog that gets hold of
a rag doll and shakes it, and shakes it,
and shakes it until what it wants
shakes out, I will put my whole heart
into whatever I care about.*

Kathleen

When Autumn is at home, I will say, "Come be my little girl." She'll put her head in my lap, and we'll talk or I'll play with her hair. Then I close my eyes and remember what it was like when she was little. In a certain sense, young children die every year. A child at one is not the same child at two or at three. You can never get that one-year-old back. That's what "Come be my little girl" is all about.

When children are little, the physical relationship is so intense. When Autumn was six months old, we began swimming together. She loved the water and would quiver with excitement when I carried her to the pool. Being in the water with her gave me such a wonderful sense of being a female animal. I felt like a mother dolphin swimming with my young. Then in the shower, she'd wrap her arms around my neck and her legs around my waist. Her naked little body would mold to mine, and the warm water would cascade over us. We were in our own world.

We have all been blessed with an abundance of love —my grandmother, my mother, my daughter, and myself— all nurturing and being nurtured by the intertwining of our roles and our lives. We have gloried in being women.

Ceramic plate by Autumn

50

Jan

When we travel, we just go. We have no plans. We'll get out
a map and say, "This looks interesting." We never travel on freeways.
We always take the secondary roads through the little towns.

A few years ago, I came home from ricing and said, "What d'ya say,
Toot? Why don't we go camping in South Dakota?" We threw
everything in the car and took off. On the way to Fort Thompson, the
car ahead of us hit a pheasant. I pulled over and backed up. Andrea
asked, "What are you doin'?" I said, "We're gonna have pheasant for
dinner!" That night, we built a wonderful fire and enjoyed roast pheasant
breast with wild rice and baked potatoes. By the end of five nights,
we were waking up to ice and snow. It was adventure; it was good.

Another night, in the middle of a
snowstorm, I said, "What d'ya say, Toot?
Let's walk around the lake?" So we bundled
up and started walking. It took us two and
a half hours to go four miles. There was
no path. We couldn't see the trees.
We trudged through snow up to our hips.
We were the only two people in the world
that night. It was a wonderful experience.

Andrea is our youngest daughter.
She was born seven years after
the other kids, at a time when
I was caring for my mother. In
fact, I was so busy concentrating
on her, I was six months pregnant
before I knew it! The day Andrea
was born, we learned that Mom's
cancer had recurred. Two days
later, Andrea and I flew to
Portland to be with her. We
returned two months later,
bringing my mother back to live
with us until she died. We put
a cot in Andrea's room so I could
take care of mom and nurse the
baby. Andrea has always been the
light of our lives. I think she was
sent to help us get through that
terrible ordeal.

Ngo

We immigrated to the United States when Tam was nine. Every fall before school starts,
I take her shopping. Each time, she wants something different. I don't understand this.
I say to her, "Why can't you wear what I bought you last year?"

Our first winter here, I bought Tam a warm hat. After a few years, she refused to wear it.
She wears ear muffs. I've asked her, "How come you don't get cold? What about your head?"
She never looks warm. I worry about her.

Although Tam was born in Vietnam, we are Chinese. When she was a baby, I hemmed triangles to fold and pin over her diaper and sewed matching tops to keep her tummy and chest warm. It's a standard style for both girls and boys during the first year.

Shahnaz

I was thirty-two when Freya was born. In a way, I have to say I grew
up alongside her. I was searching for some identity. She already had it!
I don't know where she got those skills. Perhaps I gave her enough
love and assurance. In any case, I feel she was clear about where
she was headed while I was still searching.

From the time Freya was born, her sense
of who she was seemed to be whole and direct.
It focused me. In many ways, we have been
mirrors for each other. I don't know who is
ahead of whom. I gave birth to her.
She gave birth to me.

Beth

When we all go somewhere as a family, we have to pile into several cars. Mom always rides in the "fun car," the one with the music blaring.

Jean

I can remember reading a book as a youngster about children who lived in a boxcar. With my own children, I wanted to create a home environment that would be fun and spontaneous. I've always said that I wish I had been my own child.

Beth

We do lead these brief, incredible lives and then once we're gone, who remembers? You want to believe there will be someone that knows you did something wonderful. I believe my mom watches my life. She is bearing witness so that if anyone asks, she can tell them. Just as I'm doing that for her.

Jean

When the kids were small, I was home with them. Being homebound meant our life was more slow-moving. The pace is so different for Beth.

Beth

For me, as a woman, it's important to have children. From my own experience as a mom, I've realized how often women have to choose. You can be a mother and have other passions, but it *is* hard to do both.

Elizabeth

My mother has always been my best friend, but working together has enriched our relationship. It's added a new dimension. It's not my mother saying, "I don't like your friends, Honey." It's my mother saying, "Do you think that's a good business decision?"

Donna

We *are* good friends, but I'm *still* her mother and I still tell her when I think she's wrong.

Elizabeth

There's a different kind of honesty, though, that has come from working together.

Donna

Yes, and it's a nice benefit for both of us. When you get older, no one tells you what's wrong with you anymore. They really don't. They're very nice to you. Your husband is used to you, your kids are gone, and your friends don't want to hurt your feelings. I *like* having to learn new ways to do things!

As business partners, we have to rely on each other for advice. When Elizabeth complained, "Everybody thinks I'm so young!" I said, "Well, then don't wear miniskirts!" When I didn't give a customer enough space, she told me, "Mom, you talked too much." I didn't get angry. She was right! We say these things to help each other.

Elizabeth

Sometimes we're so frank, we scare the hell out of people! Because we're mother and daughter, we can do that!

Angie

Bri was "born into" our lifestyle of nonviolent protest and hospitality for the homeless. I didn't decide to live this way *after* becoming a mother. The first time Bri saw me arrested for an act of nonviolence was very difficult. At times, her growing up in a hospitality house has not been much easier, but I have always felt that the positive aspects outweigh the negatives. It is important for her to see my work with the guests and to experience sharing her belongings and our house with people who are homeless. Over the years, listening to her needs and opinions has mellowed some of my own beliefs and actions. I am still committed to creating a more just and peaceful world for her and all children. I hope when she is older and looks back on her childhood, she will understand that some of the craziness of our lives together was rooted in this desire.

A piece of the Berlin Wall

The two of us were in Germany within weeks of the fall of the Berlin Wall. There were people everywhere, sledgehammering at the holes. Brianna turned four while we were there.

Yvonne

In the summertime, Jocelyn would go to the field and pick wild flowers: daisies, buttercups,
Indian paintbrushes, and lupines. I particularly remember the daisies. They smelled awful!
We had to put them on the table and then try to eat dinner.

Jocelyn
That was our forest. We found all sorts of things out there—strawberries, frogs, bugs, rocks.
And *everything* came home.

Jocelyn
I used to walk home from school for lunch.

Yvonne

I liked that. I had that when I was a child. That way
you could talk to your parents in the middle of the day.

Jocelyn
Sometimes, we had tomato soup and cheese sandwiches.
I had to chew my food thirty-two times before swallowing so it
would digest well. When I got to high school, I realized how
slowly I ate compared to my friends.

Kate

I assumed that once we decided to have children, it would just happen. Infertility was incredibly hard for me to accept. But once I did, we started talking about the issues of adoption. It was a topic whispered about when I was growing up. "Well, you know she was *adopted,* don't you?" Would adoption be second-best to having a biological child? I wanted to be sure I could say with an open heart and open arms, "This is *not* second best. This is by choice!"

Our baby daughter came ten years, almost to the day, after we married. Heidi knows I'm not her birth mother; I'm her life mother. I made that promise.

In our poem, "Setisoppo," or opposites spelled backwards, we are trying to look at who we are, as we are.

Sometimes we think
The other is not
What we want them to be
Setisoppo-opposites
You and Me

We *are* opposites in many ways. But what if we are? So what!

Karen

My father didn't approve of dancing. On Wednesday nights, when he went
to choir practice, my mother would haul out the Norwegian folk music,
roll up the red rug . . . and *we would dance!*

My mother has given me many gifts, one of them is the love of music.
When I was seven, the church loaned us a piano and mother somehow
managed to pay for lessons on her cook's salary. She still loves to hear me play.
I really have modest talent, but in her eyes, I can do no wrong at the piano.

*My mother was forty with four grown
children when I was born, so our relationship
has always felt grandmotherly. She is a
kind, gracious little lady, with a marvelous
sense of humor and a positive outlook on life.
She doesn't dwell on the past or worry
about the future. She is very much
"of the moment."*

Karen

Chloe's temper can be a problem, but it doesn't smolder long.
It's out there and then done with. She's very spunky.
I love that about her. I'm inclined to stuff my emotions
and let them build.

Chloe

I know that I'm emotional and have a temper.
In elementary school, I used to cry easily, which got me
teased a lot. A therapist helped me learn how to cope.
She told me to take deep breaths, count to ten,
and then evaluate the situation.

Karen

Chloe and I were alone together for the first four years
of her life. I never doubted that I could manage.

Single parenting was my
frame of reference. For awhile
it was "just the two of us
together against
the world."

1988

ork like at Camp ?!
I wish we'd hear from
you — are you having
a good time? great time.
OK time? terrible time.
I figure "no news is good
news." We're off to Quadson
today — will miss you.
Call Sunday night!
See you. love mom.

Museum Ludwig

Bestell-Nr.: ML 61

Mary

When I'm busy and Nadine comes up and wants my attention, I try to stop for that moment of need. I didn't stop and take time with my older children. I couldn't give them that moment. I didn't have it to give. I can't go back and undo. But, in a sense, Nadine is my second chance. I call her my *Chula*—my dear, beautiful, sweet girl.

"Sharing a Moment" by Mary

Simin

Jessica carries her basket of "little people" everywhere . . . to
parties, soccer games, and grandma's house. If one is missing,
she can't go on with her day. I use them to encourage her to
do things. For example, if she doesn't
want to take a bath I will say, "Let's do it for Johnny
or Bobbie or Baby. They're going to take a bath.
If you want to be with them, you have to come too."
Then she will immediately pick up the basket and come,
for they always bathe together. Each figure has a special perch.
The soap dish is a popular diving board.

I had absolutely no contact with anyone
with a disability before Jessica was born.
I grew up in Iran, where people with
disabilities disappeared. They were not
kept at home. I don't remember seeing
anyone with Down's Syndrome
around me. Once we learned to take
one-step-at-a-time, one-day-at-a-time,
our concerns about her future
became more manageable.

Crystal

Being Asian in a white family wasn't the problem. It was having my parents say you've got to do this or that. I would never listen. I had friends that didn't have rules or curfews, but I always had consequences.

Addie

Adolescence was not very kind to Crystal. Eventually, she worked herself down to "grounded with no radio, no TV, no stereo, and no phone." She sat in her room and stared out the window. When she came of age, it was incredibly difficult, at first, to put away what had gone before and trust and respect her new choices.

Although Crystal was a handful, I have yet to give her the Mother's Curse. I promised myself early on never to say, "I hope you have a child *just like you* when you grow up!" So far, I've kept my promise.

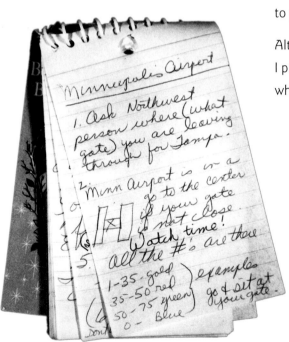

Addie

When Crystal traveled by herself to visit her grandparents, I gave her very specific instructions.

Crystal

I get lost very easily.

Addie

We say she's directionally challenged.

Kelly

Olivia's Indian name is Ge Way Du Nu Kway, or "Woman Standing North." At her naming ceremony, she was given an eagle feather to represent love. My feather was given to me by a medicine man, to take with me whenever I travel. As symbols of love and protection, our eagle feathers are part of our link—as mother and daughter and as Anishinabeg.

When Olivia was three, she asked, "Mom do you remember when you were an egg?" I laughed and said, "No. Do you?" "Oh yes!" she said, and I believe she does. Medicine people say babies are very close to the spirit world. They remember. I have a picture of my mother, who died when I was eleven. A year or two ago, Olivia looked sadly at that picture and said, "I miss Grandma Maxine. Do you?" I said, "What?"

She saw the shocked look on my face. Then, more quietly, I asked, "You miss Grandma Maxine, do you?" She said, "Yeah, I really do." It touched me that she was so moved. We've gone to her grave a couple of times. Olivia is very attuned to everything around her. I'm sure she knows my mother. I'm sure my mother visits her a lot.

Children are incredible teachers. In simple ways, they teach us lessons. Many times they address the things we don't want to look at. I'll be standing at the sink, washing dishes, and something will come from her that suddenly touches me—something I know I have to think about.

The Ojibwe word for jingle dress is ziibaaska'iganagooday. The jingles are made from my grandpa's snuff can covers. Both of my daughters have danced. Olivia loves the drum. She gets lost in it.

Judith

Mother often knew when to indulge our whims. When we moved to a new house in a new city, she said we could each choose the color to paint our bedrooms. I chose deep purple and lilac. Mother didn't protest, so my sister and I lived in purple splendor for three years.

Mary

I always told my girls that they had strong wills and, with that will, they could move mountains . . . or create havoc.

Judith

She also told me that we were to dress nicely and wear clean underwear on trips.

At bedtime, Mom would go from room to room to say "the prayer" over my sisters and me. She'd smooth her hand over my brow and recite:

> Defend oh Lord, this thy child
> With Thy heavenly grace.
> That she may continue Thine forever,
> And daily increase in Thy holy spirit,
> More and more,
> Until she comes to Thine everlasting kingdom.
> Amen

If she took too long, my sisters would call out, "Mom, are you coming to say the prayer?"

Flashbacks

Sometimes I wish I could reach back,
And talk to you then in your space.
We might not agree,
But we could share thoughts and feelings,
Talk as equals, let our guards down,
Colleagues in this business of mothering.

I'd like to know how you really coped,
With runny noses, rainy afternoons,
Children who fought and complained,
Phones jangling, moving across the country,
Three cases of the German measles,
Fragmented days, nights with no steam left.

Today you say, "Oh, it was easy . . .
You were such good children."
But how you must have worked
To strike a balance, juggle needs,
Keep the family happy,
It must have been hard as hell
To be a good wife and mother.

Judith

From an early age, music fueled her. As an infant, she sat on the bed
while I practiced my violin. At two, Kirsten would swing and sway
on the sunlit patio, dancing with her whole body. At three, she sang
her favorite record, "Free to Be You and Me," to her dolls. Today we
still share a love of music. Music links me to her, just as it links
my mother to me.

Kirsten

When Mom would leave for orchestra
rehearsals, I would run and kiss her at
the door. She always wore lipstick,
so I'd get lipstick on my cheek and,
for a minute, be drowned in the scent
of her perfume.

Dear
Mom,
Please do not feed
the fish. I think
I have to much school
work! I'm being
pressed. I love you!
Also Dad, Please
treat me older than
Erika! Say good night.

Love,
Kirsten

P.S.
Turn off the fish light
an lock the doors and make
sure the lights are turned
out! I miss writing these!

Jan

I knew how important Cabbage Patch dolls were to Sarah. I made
the doll, the bunny slippers, the jogging suits, and all the other
outfits to show her just how much I loved her. The first thing she
did when I gave it to her was pull down the pants to check for the
Cabbage Patch label. She was so disappointed!
At her age, it wasn't the real thing without
the official label. She had no concept
of what it took to make that doll.
Ironically, what started out as a
rejected gift later became "Kaitlin,"
a favorite companion.

Recently, we ran across a
photograph of me smiling, hands
covered with flour, creating
something in the kitchen. Sarah said,
"*That's* how I remember you." Then she
added, "It's so different than my image of
you today." Together, we've moved through tragedy and loss.
As a widow, I've become Sarah's sole provider. Her image of me
today includes a daily planner and a cellular phone. I'm very much
the corporate woman I need to be.

Sarah is very different
than I am. I'm a fast,
make-the-list-and-check-
it-off kind of person.
She is more deliberate.
I have had to learn to pace
myself in a way that allows
her to be herself.
We have an incredible
relationship. We're not
the "Partridge Family,"
but we do practice
mutual respect.

Cynthia

Angilea was so ready for college. I felt weepy about the distance that would soon separate us. It didn't take me long to realize that her absence was a mixture of sadness and relief. Once she was away at school, I slept differently. When she came home on breaks, my internal clock would kick in and there I'd be, wide awake, waiting up. She would go back to school and z-z-z-z-z. I was so tuned into her rhythms. I'm still learning to let go.

One of the reasons Angilea was such a good kid was, after watching me deal with twenty troubled foster children in our home, she was clear about what my limits were. She never tested them. I wasn't a hard disciplinarian, but I was firm. Sometimes, other kids would come to stay because their parents felt secure about the boundaries at our house. We talked about boundaries as mutual respect. I, too, would leave a note as to where I was going, would call if I was running late. Those were house rules.

We searched high and low for a minister who would perform an ecumenical baptismal service. My mom, my grandmother, and Angilea's godparents were present for the christening. The pastor used a small baptismal pitcher containing blessed water from Minnehaha Falls.

"We rejoice that in her birth, and the birth of all babies now taking place across this planet, the human race begins again. What has not been invades the structure of what is with ten thousand countenances. Angilea's life helps us to hope again."

—Pastor Richard McNeill

Dianne

We're not a musical family, but I was not swayed by that fact. Krista started clarinet lessons in the second grade. Well, she wouldn't practice! She wouldn't practice alone, and she wouldn't let me help. Amid shrieking, the clarinet was slammed up into a storage space and laid aside! She tried it again in the fourth grade but never had much success. Krista and I agree that this clarinet is certainly about us: the arguing, my failure to find a way to get her to practice, her absolute stubbornness, my lack of perspective, and then the second effort with no better results. As parents, what we want for our kids and what they want gets all jumbled together.

Giving Krista a sense of belonging to the whole world is important to me. The world is populated with individuals who are intrinsically of equal worth. We don't understand this here in our country. Remember during the Vietnam War, it was said that one American life was worth ten Vietnamese? I think the path to understanding is to know people from other countries, to know how to operate in foreign countries, and to speak their languages. I wanted to give each of my children a safe foreign travel experience. Krista and I have biked together through the German countryside near Billerbeck.

We spent hours and hours and hours reading to our children. Krista has always loved books. She used to read during her classes in school. It was the same thing on school nights at home. One of her tricks was to read with the flashlight under the covers at night. She got her flashlight confiscated. Then it was reading with the lamp. She got the lamp confiscated. One night, I came home around eleven o'clock and saw that Krista had her light on! I took the step ladder up to her quickly-darkened room and unscrewed the light bulb from her ceiling light.

Karen

I believe that mothering is about a relationship, not about a role. It's something you do *with* not *over and against* a child. My sister has said I treat my children as if they were my grandchildren. In a sense, she's right. I do have this ability to separate and let Sarah have her own experience. On the other hand, I will say hard things when necessary. I *treasure* my daughter because I find her to be an interesting person, but I have never felt any obligation to *like* her all of the time.

Sarah is wonderful—blending in, adjusting, flexing-pushing, at times, the line between charming and obnoxious—so like me I think.

Journal excerpt from June 29, 1987

Wanda

My mother remembers every detail of my Quinceañera,
my fifteenth birthday celebration, beginning with the
150 invitations. On that day, we walked with relatives
and friends to the church for the Father's blessing.
I had fifteen attendants dressed in magenta pink.
I wore a crown and a white dress. There was dancing,
with a special waltz in my honor. The fact that I live in
Minnesota and my mother still lives in Puerto Rico
makes us both sad. We talk by phone at night,
every other week.

Se realiza la ilusión
de mis años juveniles!
Con júbilo y emoción,
celebremos mis quince abriles!

Sitio Casa de Wandy
Fecha 22/6/81
Hora 8 P.M.
Nombre Wanda Pacheco

INVITACION A FIESTA
DE UNA QUINCEAÑERA

Wanda

Joannie plays baseball on Monday and Wednesday nights, and I will not miss a game. I taught her how to bat. The first time she hit the ball, I started screaming, "Go, Joannie, go!" She waved her hands as if to say, "Calm down, Mom. Can't you see my friends are here?"

I'm teaching Joannie the same manners my mother taught me when I was a little girl in Puerto Rico. At her age, she still looks to me for approval. "Is this okay for me to do, Mom?" I want my daughter to finish school and *then* get married! I want her to have goals instead of babies so young. That's why I tell her to "look around before taking a step."

Joannie's First Communion

Joannie was born in Minnesota. She and I learned English together, watching Big Bird on Sesame Street. She's bilingual, but speaks Spanish with an American accent! She tells her cousins in Puerto Rico, "I'm Minneso-Rican."

Lonni

Sue never *asks* for my advice as much as she *listens* for my reactions. She took complete charge of her own wedding. She even picked out *my* dress. The only thing I remember doing is . . . I can't remember a thing!

At the time of our portrait, I wasn't thinking, "Oh, thank God I'm going to be a grandmother." I had no idea if I would like being one. I was just so pleased for her, and proud too. I had helped her grow up to be what she always wanted to be, a mother.

When you're busy raising children, it's hard to stand back far enough to watch those precious lives evolve. Parenting is a lot of work for a long time. Those who want instant gratification, shouldn't have children. The dividends do come, but much later.

Learning to play music is part of our family heritage, although I'm talking about a family that's not musical at all! It was a given: children and music lessons. With Sue, the lessons took. "Moonlight Sonata" had been my last recital piece. When Sue learned to play it, she added a new layer to my memories. It pleases me to have that musical connection.

Sue

Becoming a mother gave me a whole new purpose in life. I want Bridget to associate her mommy with unconditional love and security. There is somebody completely devoted to her happiness—me.

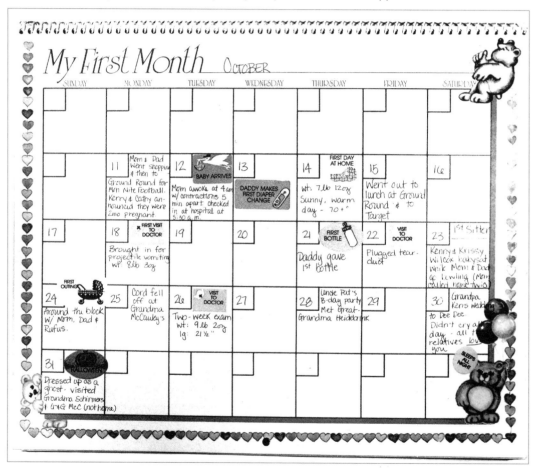

Doris

The older I grow the more beautiful the world becomes. The sky appears more blue, the trees a darker, more lustrous green. Even the highways brighten. I suspect it is because my vision is growing dimmer that I magnify the color in my surroundings.

I have memories of the woods surrounding. We always went to Glen Avon in the spring of the year to watch the cascading foamy water rush down the rocks and send a cold spray into our faces. It seemed to me that no other place on earth was more beautiful in its solitary splendor.

Should I go blind someday, I will carry these memories with me with others I gleaned from our travels. I will call upon them from that special compartment of my mind to refresh my spirit.

Journal entry, March 3, 1988

Julie

Due to the effects of lifelong diabetes, my mother gradually lost her vision and experienced *complete* darkness the last seven years of her life. She made it seem pretty easy to be blind even though I'm sure it wasn't. That was the way she was about everything that happened to her in her life.

I've returned from our four day canoe trip
to the Boundary Waters with the call of
the wild in heart. Last night I walked in
the darkness, down to the water's edge. It
was calm and warm and bugless. I was
delighted and gifted to see in the waters
reflected the big dipper and other stars.
Everything was so bright and wonderful.
A loon called and another loon
answered . . .

Journal entry, August 14, 1987

*My mom collected cups and saucers; she liked to set
a nice table. Now I find I'm the same way even
though I don't want to be! I find myself gravitating
toward table things. A nice table with nice linens and
dishes seems important to me now.*

Ann

My parents were married for ten years before
I was born. My sense is I was a cherished child.
On the other hand, every time I moved past a
milestone, there was a sort of sadness.

One of the most amazing things about my
mother is her letter-writing. She keeps in touch
with people from seventy years ago. Sometimes,
as you get older, your world tends to get smaller.
But through her letter-writing, my mother is
enjoying friendships that were started
decades ago. I've come to realize the gift
of communication. That's why, every year,
I send out 250 Christmas cards!

One of the gifts my mother gave to me was
an awareness that she was a unique, distinct
individual with her own identity. I never had the
sense of her fading into the background.

Anns curls the first time her hair was cut!

Through a Daughter's Eyes
She treasured her pen:
black with chrome trim,
surface luring reflections.
We were in big trouble if it disappeared.
I couldn't understand why a pen was so important.
It was one of those first things
that made me think
maybe
my mother was a separate person.

by Ann

Ann

Starting in late elementary school, sometimes as often as weekly, Rachel asked me questions about her handicap. Sometimes it was only one question. Sometimes it would be a whole series of questions. My answer was usually just like the last time she asked the question. I'd occasionally get irritated at the repetition, but I understood she was grappling with the same mystery.

Rachel

When did you know I had a handicap?

Ann

At about one year when you didn't walk alone.

Rachel

How did you feel about that?

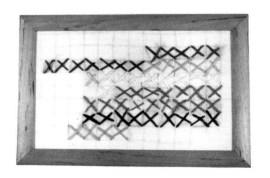

Ann

We wished you didn't have to deal with this, but you were still the same daughter we loved.

Rachel

What would I be like if I didn't have a handicap?

Ann

I guess the same, except with less frustration.

Rachel

Where did I get my (eyes, height, sense of humor, or any of twenty different things)? From you or from Dad?

Ann

It's hard to say. You're a mixture of both of us.

Rachel

Why am I handicapped?

The cross-stitch project represents our joint efforts to understand and channel her special gifts in ways that weren't frustrating. Once she had those access points, she experienced her own skills and developed along her own path.

Ruth

As the youngest of three daughters, I had lots of freedom
and no curfew. I never gave cause. I never gave reason.
I didn't take risks or live on the edge. I was the "Good Kid"
until I hit my thirties. Then I rocked the boat . . . in a Swedish way.

Evelyn

When Ruth got divorced, I worried that, as a parent, I didn't do
enough or I did too much! That's the first thing I did. I blamed myself!

Ruth

Do you still take the blame?

Evelyn

You bet I don't! I've shed that one!

*My mom has always worked with her
hands—needlepoint, sewing, and knitting.
Early on, I learned from her that one way to
relieve stress is to get out of your head and
move your hands.*

Ruth

We drove 150 miles to find the fabric, and I combined three different patterns to create the design. I sewed the prom dress of her dreams, or so I thought. From Kiki's perspective, it was never quite perfect. I altered that dress four or five times ... the rib cage was wrong, the bodice, the hem, the straps. By the time I was done, I thought, "This is nuts! I'll never sew for her again!" She may never wear the dress again, but I'll never get rid of it. It's too symbolic.

Without Kiki, there wouldn't have been a mirror for me. We're both Scorpios and kid about how intense and passionate we are. At bedtime, I would massage her head, draw pictures on her back, help her to breathe deeply and visualize clouds. It was very calming for both of us.

Bobbie

Since she was old enough to tell me, Sarah will only wear one kind of socks, and only one store carries them. I cannot get any other type of socks on her feet. She has worn them in various sizes her entire life. There will never be other socks until she's old enough to wonder, "Will people make fun of me if I continue to wear lace on my ankles?" On the other hand, when I do the laundry, I never have odd socks!

We've always been "girls on the go." If Sarah misbehaved at my mother-in-law's house, we would head for the bathroom, where I would go nose-to-nose with her. Keeping my voice very low, I went through the "if you ever do that again" routine. She'd slowly back right up to the toilet saying, "Okay, okay!" From then on, she would behave. To this day, my mother-in-law does not know what happened in that bathroom. But now, when other grandchildren misbehave, she says," Well, why not take them to the bathroom?"

When I think about my hopes and dreams for Sarah, there's my knee-jerk reaction and the big picture one. Knee-jerk? I hope she marries just one person and it works out, that she has a successful marriage. The big picture? It's very important for her to have a trade, an occupation or profession. I don't care if she's a bricklayer. It's just important that she have something for herself that's hers, like I have. That's the big picture. But my heart tells me, one person, one marriage, a good relationship.

Delilah

During graduate school, my sexual identity became clear to me. My mother was the first person I told. "Mom," I said, "I think I'm bisexual." She said, "I'm sure you're *wholly* sexual, and I'm so proud of you!" The support was that fast.

Susan

Wherever Delilah has lived, I've visited and vacationed. We get together at least twice a year.

Delilah

Many times I'll be planning things and think, "I'll save that until Mom comes."

Delilah

Any letter that I receive from my mother has loads of newspaper clippings. For ten years she has kept me up to date with hometown news.

Marjorie

My father, Chief of the Sac and Fox Tribe in Oklahoma, died when I was fourteen. With modest means, my mother was determined to continue life as it had been before we lost Dad. We lived out in the country and raised cattle. During the winter, she would go down to the pond and crack the ice so the cattle could drink. She'd feed them every morning before leaving for her job as a bookkeeper. Quite often, the cattle would get out and the neighbors would call her at work. I look back on that time now, and I don't know how she did it.

My mother is a strong woman. She was widowed at the age of forty-two with three children. She will tell you, "My children have been my life." She always let us know we were very special. She would say, "Someone is going to be the leader, so it might as well be you!" She pushed us to excel; she's still pushing. At her age, we really don't know how long we have with her. I can't imagine her not being here. I do know that this is the time to be extra nice, to take extra care of her for this is the "long good-bye."

Carolyn

Mary was my fourth pregnancy but our first child to live beyond
a few minutes. Her four-month ultrasound picture indicated she was
developing normally. It was a very good moment, one of our best.

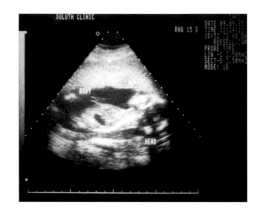

Mary was born six weeks early; she wanted into this world!

Mary was named after my mother, Mary, who died when I was thirty.
She had told me that one of the saddest things that can happen is to
have your mom die young. I stood over her grave and said, "You're right."

There's a certain silence I remember on the day my mom died, walking
into her house. It was the same silence I had when we lost our first
daughter. I never got to bring her home. I walked into that house and it
was quiet. There's a sound that would never be heard there.

My mother's best friend knit this set for her when she was pregnant with me. When I was pregnant with Mary, mom pulled it out for "good luck." During the pregnancy, I had two surgeries but all ended well. This outfit is a piece of my mom's history, my history, and now Mary's history. I secretly hope that when she has a girl, her daughter will come home from the hospital in it, too.

Angela

After my parents divorced, it was really hard watching her.
Mom was scared of being alone. My brother and I were
there, but we were moving on. Gradually, she took charge
of everything. I was impressed. I watched her develop a
whole new life. In some ways, it might have helped our
relationship. It gave us the distance we needed.
We became more separate, but in a positive way.

Judy

Orange Drop Cookies is a four-generation recipe that
begins with my grandmother. It's in my mother's
handwriting. My mother died in a car accident when
I was twenty-six. I felt cheated to lose her so early, so
I always try to hang on to anything in her handwriting.
I can remember helping with the cookies
as a little girl . . . frost and eat, frost and eat.

RECIPE FOR Orange Drop Cookies

INGREDIENTS

1½ cups sugar
1 cup Crisco + butter
grated rind + juice of 1 orange
1 cup sour milk
1 tsp Soda
1 tsp Baking powder
3½ cups sifted flour
1 egg

PREPARATION AND COOKING INSTRUCTIONS add
Cream sugar + shortening egg + beat
Add juice + rind until
" Sour milk
" Flour + Soda B.P. sifted
together — Drop from tsp about
2 inches apart - they spread when
baking - Bake about 11 min at
350° - Icing - melted
Butter - juice of orange and
powdered sugar to make stiff -

MAKES   SERVINGS

Erika
When I go to bed, Pink Blankie goes too.

Sue

Pink Blankie goes over her first and *then* the sheet,
even in the summer. The blanket came from my
Grandma Thompson, who died shortly after Erika
was born. Although they never met, Pink Blankie
touches both generations.

Bedtime takes an hour. We brush her teeth, read
stories, and then cuddle. After I tuck her in, and start
down the hall, Erika will call out, "One more hug!"
Halfway down the steps, she'll say, "Mom, one
more kiss!" Finally, I say, "No, that's it.
It's eight o'clock. Good night."
"Just one more" happens every night.

Judy

Childhood memories of fleeing the Nazis have impacted my mothering style. At the beginning of World War II, my family got a warning from the milkman that we should leave Copenhagen. I remember skipping home from school, and my mother telling me that we had to leave. Everything was left as it was: the mop in the bucket and the houselights on.

Even though we were war refugees, my mother made sure I was always neat and clean. A lot of times, that meant washing at night or every other night the one outfit I had. I grew up on hand-me-downs. She made snowsuits out of draperies, dresses out of sheets. When Cindy was young, I liked to dress her in white and wouldn't let her get dirty. Isn't that terrible? When she was two and a half, I hand-knit a special skirt and sweater for her to wear. To this day, she loves clothes, and shopping is something that she and I really like to do together.

Cindy's my best friend. I have always stressed "family first." There's nothing in life more important. Mother's Day is traumatic for Cindy, who lost triplets at six months. I know how painful those memories still are for her.

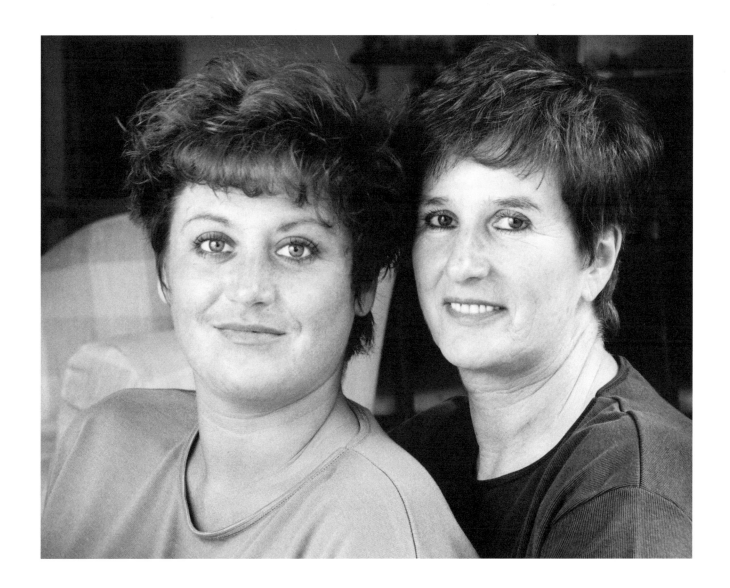

Normajean

To see girls in ponytails, carrying their own sports bags and wearing their *own* sports jackets has been a tremendous satisfaction. For a girl to suit up with a team, to belong, to get out there, is a learning experience—a great way to channel energy. I didn't have that experience. That Annelise could have this opportunity has been pure joy.

I don't know how I got her to agree to the portrait in the first place! At fifteen, anything your mother wants you to do is probably stupid. She was very resistant. But that's what daughters need to do. Her reaction to the portrait? "I don't like my hair!"

Looking into the portrait for the first time, I wept. My hand is on her shoulder while she moves forward, emerging. I need to be close while she is pulling away. This journey of letting go is very intense. The portrait describes us . . . push and pull, darkness and light.

Dearest Mom,
I don't know what to get for you or what to do for you. Just tell me what you'd like. I love you so much. I'm glad you found your checkbook.

love,
Annelise

Annelise often sat at her little table and chair while I wrote in my journal. She would copy what I did. We lit our writing candles, and she would draw pictures.

Carmen

I make coffee for my Mom every morning. I measure five scoops into the filter and add three cups of water. Before she can drink it, I take a blood sample from her finger and check it on the machine. The numbers should be above 100. If they're lower, she needs sugar.

Marilyn

It was my doctor who suggested I teach the children how to check my blood sugar. Carmen has been helping me since she was nine years old.

At night, I say "Good night" and my Mom says, "Dios te bendiga" or God bless you.

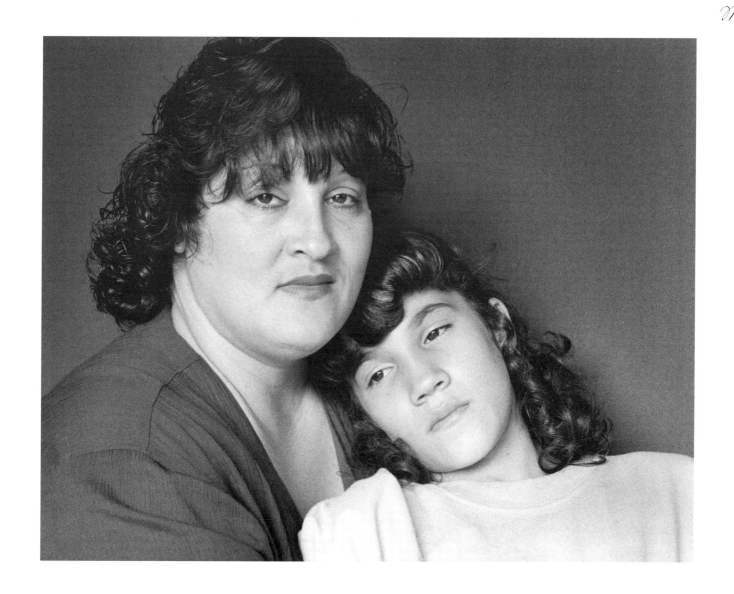

Nancy

Lisa grew up as a country girl. She had chores.
We worked right alongside one another. We spent
summers training our horses, riding them back and
forth to a swimming hole down the road. We had
cows, pigs, and chickens too. Come fall, we butchered
and put up hay. In winter, the two of us would axe the
frozen "horse cookies" in the stalls. This was our way
of life together until she was seventeen.

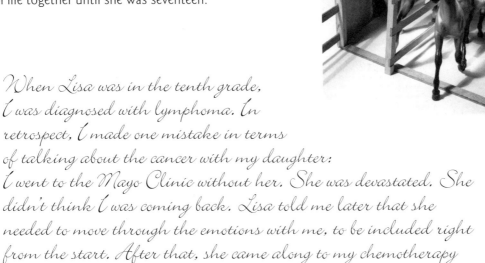

When Lisa was in the tenth grade,
I was diagnosed with lymphoma. In
retrospect, I made one mistake in terms
of talking about the cancer with my daughter:
I went to the Mayo Clinic without her. She was devastated. She
didn't think I was coming back. Lisa told me later that she
needed to move through the emotions with me, to be included right
from the start. After that, she came along to my chemotherapy
sessions and helped take care of me.

Nhia

I grew up in a small village in Laos. I asked my parents many times if I could attend school, but they did not want me to go. They knew of only one person in the village who was thought to be educated. After his schooling, he had come back a poor man with no farming skills. When I was fifteen, I asked again, just as I had done every year I can remember. This time they agreed, but soon my brother and I fled to Thailand because of the war in our country.

Three years later, my husband and I came to the United States as refugees. I have recently returned to school. My dream for Amanda is that she will have a good education. She speaks English and Hmong and loves to sing and dance. I tell her, "Amanda, someday you will be a good teacher."

Linda

When I was pregnant with Sarah, I kept wondering how I could possibly love this child as much as I loved our first daughter. And then she got here, and I thought she was so amazing! Because she was the second child, I loosened up. I said, "Hey, I'm just going to have fun with this one." With the first child, I was so earnest. Parenting the "right way" took over. With Sarah, I managed to capture the joy.

I was always taken by Sarah's sweetness. I had trouble getting mad at her. However, when Sarah was two, we went through a year of bad tantrums. "No" wasn't something she dealt with very well. I was told that what your child is like at two is what she will be like as a teenager. Was that true? I decided I couldn't possibly handle a teenager who would act that way! When she had a temper tantrum, I sat and held her the entire time, repeating, "It's still 'no' and I love you."

Sandra

When Brynnetta was a baby, her dad died. I was a college student. Until she was almost three, her favorite place to be was on my chest. We had a study ritual. I'd hold my book above me and read to her whatever I was studying.

Brynnetta

I still remember. I remember that sensation of being on your chest, feeling your breath. That was such a tranquil, warm feeling.

Sandra

The day Brynnetta got married, I called Brad on the phone and gave him the mother-in-law talk. I told him he was very special, that I loved him very much, that I couldn't have chosen a nicer person to marry my daughter, and that, in our family, we believe that you love and pamper your women. If he felt he couldn't do that, he needed to step away. As long as he treated my daughter well, *he* would be treated well. If he mistreated her, he'd have trouble on his hands. I also told him that we don't have in-laws. He's my son, and I would treat him that way.

Brynnetta

I'd already given him that talk. I was ready for some pampering!

When I graduated and moved to Arizona, my mother sent me a card that said, "You're terrific!" I still carry the card in my wallet. It signifies what an optimistic person my mom is. Sometimes I tend to be moody and feel that life is unkind. But my mom has always been a positive force, helping me see the bright side. She will say, "If you think you can, or if you think you can't, you're absolutely right!"

134

Lyn

As adults, we have discovered that we have similar concerns and passions: working for peace and justice, enjoying the environment, and discovering other cultures. We wear on our ears what we believe about the world. The earrings that we give to each other carry special meanings.

Sarah

We also have the same tendency to "always try to do one more thing" before we leave the house. It's a predictable pattern. We're both always late.

Lyn

Our visits together bring closeness, as well as tension. Before a visit, Sarah is full of anticipation and the desire "to connect." After a day or two of being home, I sense her tension. I know she feels wedged between loyalties—familiar family patterns versus those established with her husband. When they're leaving, I find it difficult to let go and say good-bye. But as soon as they're gone, I vacuum and get the house in order, and life goes on!

Amy

When I think back to my relationship with my mom, I divide it into two areas: before she was sick and during her death. Before her illness we traveled together, baked Christmas cookies every year, went out to the movies or to dinner. I'd call her to help me shop for clothes. It's stuff like that I keep bumping into. I miss being the best of friends.

The role reversal was hard for me. My mom always took care of me. She was my mom. Then her need for care outweighed mine. I was angry at times. I wanted my mom to take care of me again, even for a little while. I'm happy that I was able to give that to her, but it was hard. That wasn't the way it was supposed to be.

Both of my maternal grandparents died of cancer, very soon after their diagnoses. When my mother found out *she* had cancer, her first thought was, "I only have a few months to live." *My* thought was, "What's the treatment?" When you're young, you think you're immortal. The older you get the more mortal you feel. My mom's death still strikes me as a fluke. She was so young.

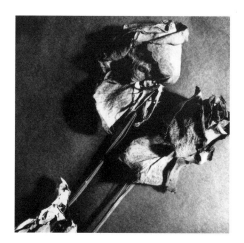

*I've kept a couple of roses from one of the
floral arrangements at the memorial service.
Actually, they've just been sitting out on my porch.
I don't really know what to do with them
but I just can't bear to throw them away.*

138

Audrey

When trying new things, you have to sound excited. The first time I gave Charlotte a teaspoon of green beans, I waved it in the air with a big smile on my face and said, "Mmm, Momma's favorite!" As soon as I put it in her mouth, she hated it. But each time, it got harder and harder for her to resist because there was Mom, still dancing with that spoonful of beans. Now she loves green beans! It's the same thing with books. I introduced Charlotte to books at five months, describing both in English and Korean what was on each page. I want her to think of books as fun.

I'm 100% certain our patterns get passed from mother to daughter. A day doesn't go by that I don't say, "Where did she get that?" But I know where Charlotte gets her traits. They didn't start with me, nor will they end with her. I'm sure the patterns came from my mother and her mother before her.

The great thing about being a woman in this culture is that there are no official limits. My mother didn't say to me, "Be a surgeon." Instead, she said, "You are capable of doing it." Then I chose to become one. It's not the specific occupation, but the belief that you can reach out and do what it is you want to do! That's what my mother gave to me and what I will pass on to Charlotte.

빤 짝 빤 짝 작은 별
아름답게 빛이네
동쪽 하늘 에서도
서쪽 하늘 에서도
빤 짝 빤 짝 작은 별
아름답게 빛이네.

Twinkle, twinkle little star . . .

Reflections

Divergent paths and inextricable bonds coexist in mother-daughter histories. Each of us continues to discover, in our own way and from our own perspective, what it means to be a daughter or a mother. You are welcome to attach your own mementos and photos and to express your thoughts, wishes, or questions on the following special pages reserved just for you.

Reflections

& Connections